ROTHBURY
and
COQUETDALE

by
FRANK GRAHAM

1982

I.S.B.N. 0 85983 092 6

NORTHERN HISTORY BOOKLET No. 65

Published by FRANK GRAHAM
6 Queen's Terrace, Newcastle upon Tyne, NE2 2PL

Printed by Howe Brothers (Gateshead) Ltd.

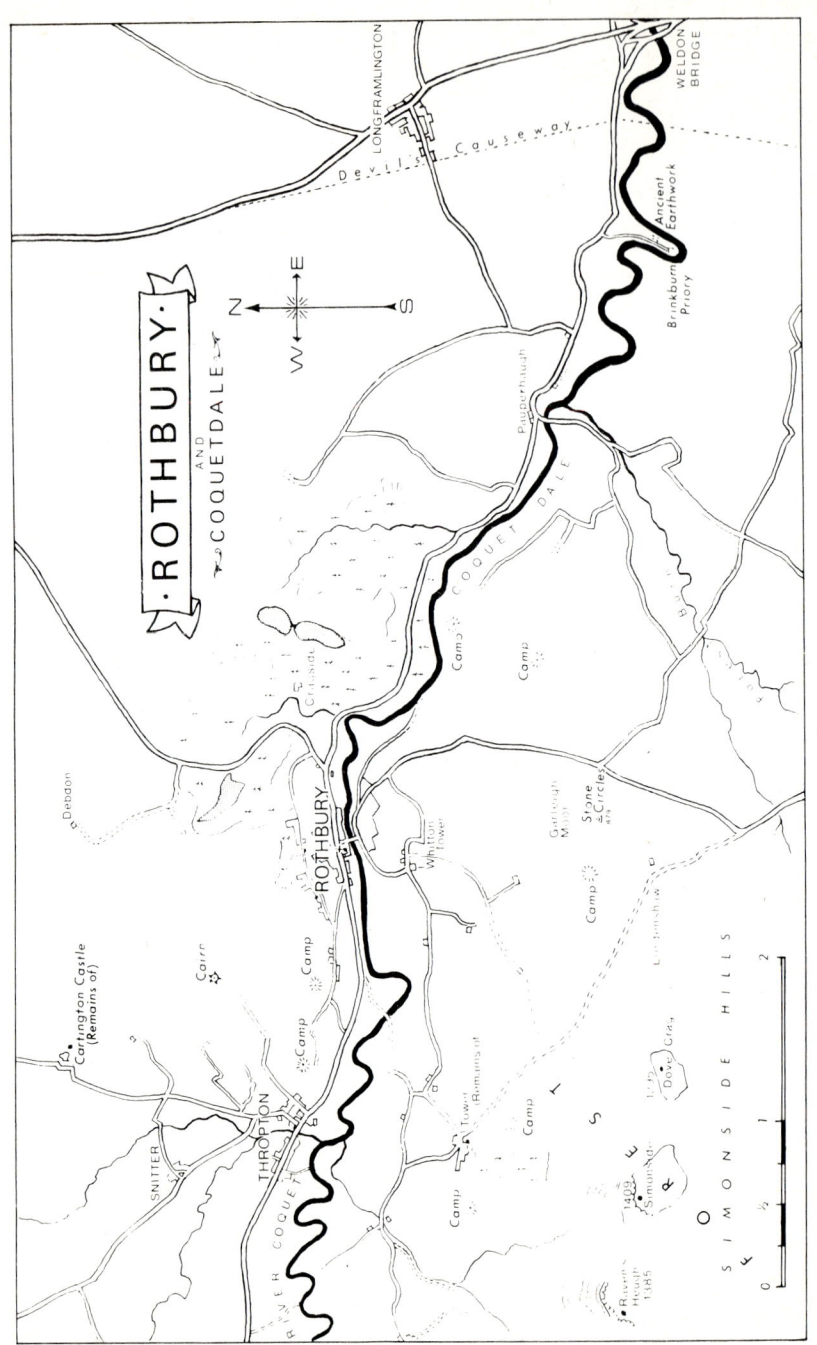

CONTENTS

	page
Rothbury	4
Old Rothbury	10
Lordenshaws	10
Rothbury Castle	11
Rothbury Forest	11
Thrum Mill	13
Weldon Bridge	15
Brinkburn Priory	15
Cragside	21
Fallowlees	27
Pauperhaugh	28
Holystone	28
Peels	29
Hepple	30
Clennell	31
Harbottle	31
Alwinton	34
Netherton	35
Snitter	35
Warton	35
Flotterton	36
Thropton	36
Whitton Tower	36
Sharp's Folly	38
Brinkheugh	38
Cartington Castle	39
Great Tosson Tower	39
Geological Walk	41
Coquetdale Sayings	44
General Information	45
The Historian of Coquetdale	45

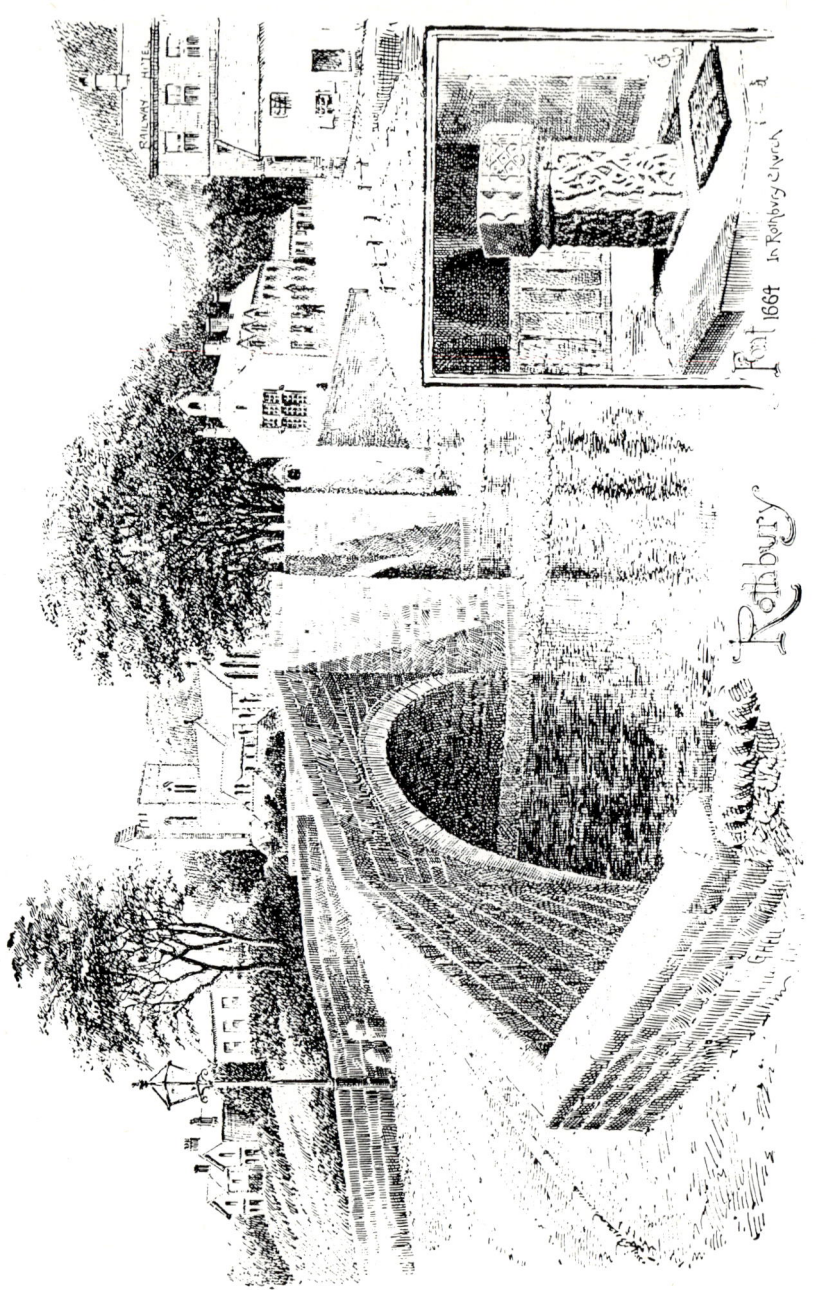

Rothbury lies on the north bank of the famous fishing stream the Coquet. The capital of Coquetdale as it has been called is almost surrounded by heather-clad and wooded hills. It is first mentioned c. 1100 as *Routhebiria* which means "Routha's town". Of pre-conquest Rothbury only the Anglian cross in the church survives. For more than a century after the Conquest the town was in the possession of the Crown. It wasn't until 1204 that King John handed it over to the lords of Warkworth. When a Norman baron obtained possession of a manor he usually erected a fortress there. Tradition says that the castle of Rothbury used to stand on the "Haa-Hill" which overlooks the Coquet fifty yards south-west of the parish church. Not a trace remains today.

In 1760 Bishop Pocock describes Rothbury as follows:—

"Rothbury is a poor town of two streets which are not paved, and the houses are mostly thatched; they cover them with sods for warmth, and thatch with heath, which will last thirty years. There are turnpike roads from it to Hexham, Newcastle, Morpeth, and Alnwick, which make it a thoroughfare from all the villages to the west and north and from Ellesden, for there is no other town this way to the west or north; the rise of the Coquet which is pronounc'd Cocket, being the bounds of Scotland at about twelve miles distance. It is a market town and they have some fairs chiefly for black cattle; and wool is sent from this place to Newcastle. They have several shops and handicrafts exercised here, particularly that of hatters. The living is in the gift of the Bishop of Carlisle and £500 a year, so that 'tis often made an option by the Archbishop of York. The parsonage house is an old tower-castle with an addition to it. Near it, the late incumbent, Dr. Sharp, prebendary of Durham, built a round tower about 30 feet high, with battlements at top from which, they say, there is a prospect of the sea. I went half a mile down the river to see the Thrum where the river falls about 40 yards through a narrow passage between the rocks about five feet wide. The salmon comes here in November to spawn, but they are not permitted to take them".

Near the church once stood the famous hostelry of the *Three Half Moons* which was in ruins in 1903. It was the principal inn of the village "where public meetings, courts of justice, courts leet and excise sittings were held, and under whose ancient and hospitable roof foregathered all classes, from the peasant to the peer, and where many a convivial party made themselves merry until 'some wee, short hour ayont the twal', in those easy going days of the past". The sign was taken from the arms of the Ogles, lords of Hepple.

Our drawing by J. T. Dixon shows the inn as it appeared in 1840, a single story building with attics, its roof covered with turf and thatched with heather, large smoking chimneys and a fine sign standing in front.

ROTHBURY, 1840. The jacket cover is based on this engraving.

Rothbury today consists of a long wide street called High Street or Front Street and two shorter streets—Rotten Row or Bridge Street and Church Street. As a market town (Charter obtained in 1291) Rothbury had a market cross erected in 1722. Unfortunately, in spite of public protests it was demolished in 1827. In 1902 an Anglian Cross was erected on the spot to the memory of Lord and Lady Armstrong. This uninteresting monument is a poor substitute for the old market cross it replaces.

Whitton Pant, Rothbury.

The Parish Church is supposed to stand on the site of a former Saxon edifice. With the exception of the chancel it was almost entirely rebuilt in 1850. Our engraving shows the church before restoration. The whole of the chancel, the east wall of the south transept and the lofty chancel arch are portions that remain of the thirteenth century building.

ROTHBURY CHURCH,
North*d*.

~ Rothbury Cross ~
Height of Shaft ~ 11ft 9ins. Total Height 15ft.1in.

But the greatest treasure in the church is the font. Though the panelled bowl is dated 1664 the stem or pedestal once formed part of a pre-conquest Saxon cross of red sandstone with fine carvings. The other portion is preserved in Newcastle. One of its broader sides is filled with an intricate knot-work pattern characteristic of that period. The other shows a mutilated figure of Christ holding a scroll in his left hand, ascending on a cloud held by angels; below are the eleven disciples and the four evangelists with their books in front. It is stated that this is the earliest carved representation in England of the Ascension of Christ and is influenced by continental carvings. On one narrow face are carved sinuous lions preying and feeding on each other with a seated human figure beneath. On the opposite side are the branches of a tree bearing berries in clusters of three. Intertwined are two animals.

The church is associated with Bernard Gilpin, Rector of Houghton-le-Spring. who in the sixteenth century travelled the north preaching to the people. He usually took the opportunity of "Christmas holydays when, on account of frost and snow, other men were loath to travel, for he found at these times the people would more usually assemble". The following incident is related by his biographer:— "Uppon a time when Mr. Gilpin was in these parts at a towne called Rothbury, there was a pestilent faction amongst some of them that were wont to resort to that church. The men being bloodily-minded, practised a bloody manner of revenge, termed by them Deadly-feod. If the faction on the one side did perhaps come to the church, the other side kept away, because they were not accustomed to meet together without bloodshed. Now, so it was, when Mr. Gilpin was in the pulpit in that church, both parties came to church and both of them stood, the one of them in the upper part of the church, or chancell, the other in the body thereof, armed with swords and javelins in their hands. Their weapons made a clashing sound, and the one side drew nearer to the other, so that they were in danger to fall to blowes in the middest of the church. Hereupon Mr. Gilpin commeth down from the pulpit, and stepping to the ring-leaders of either faction first of all he appeased the tumult. Next, he laboureth to establishe peace betwixt them, but he could not prevail in that; onely they promised to keepe the peace unbroken so long as Mr. Gilpin should remain in the Church." On another occasion he observed a glove hanging up in the church, and was informed by the sexton that it was meant as a challenge to anyone that should take it down. Gilpin ordered the sexton to reach it to him, but, upon that functionary's refusal to touch it, he removed it himself, and put it in his breast. He continued his sermon with an attack on their barbarous and inhuman customs.

One of W. B. Scott's frescoes at Wallington Hall represents this scene. We are told that one day his horse was stolen but the thief discovering whose it was immediately returned it fearing that the devil would seize him had he carried it off knowing it to be Mr. Gilpin's.

In the extension to the churchyard is the unusual headstone of "Walter Mavin, the Coquet Angler, born 1814, died 1899.

Near Rothbury are several prehistoric camps the best being Old Rothbury and Lordenshaws.

OLD ROTHBURY

The camp of Old Rothbury is half a mile N.W. of Rothbury. It occupies a strong position on the range of hills which encircle the village. It is covered with bracken but traces can be seen of a double ditch and rampart. Below the camp is the disused Pennystane Quarry where the flat penny stanes, forerunners of iron quoits, were made. Below is the smaller Westhills camp where there are traces of an outer rampart and inner rampart rising six feet.

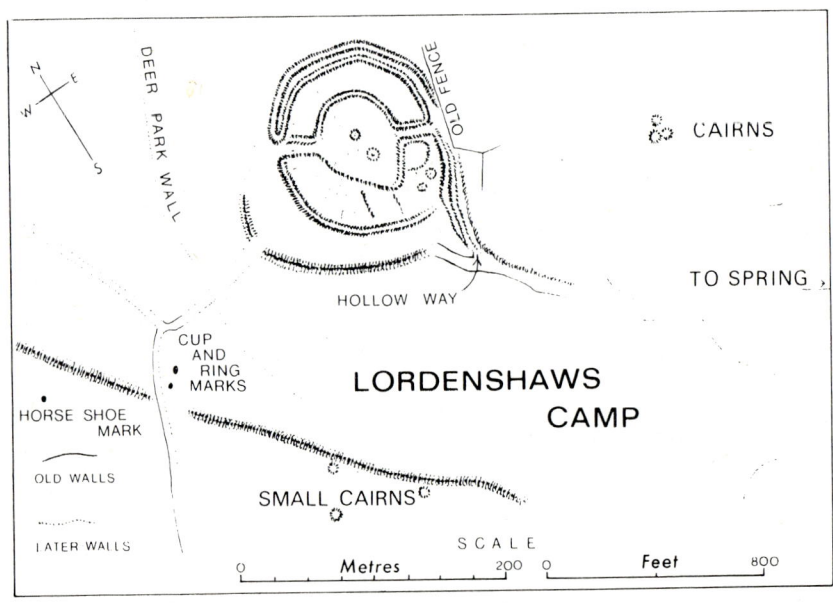

LORDENSHAWS

Lordenshaws Camp (Lower-dean-shaws) lies two miles from Rothbury, near Whitton Tower and is a fine prehistoric British camp. It stands on one of the westernmost heights of the Simonside range at a height of 879 feet, is circular in form, defended by three ramparts and a fosse. Two watch towers in connection with this camp are on Garleigh Hill to the south east and three others on the three most elevated points of the Simonside range. Our sketch shows the prehistoric remains to be seen at Lordenshaws.

Rothbury Bridge and Castle

ROTHBURY CASTLE

For more than a century after the Conquest Rothbury was in the possession of the Crown. It wasn't until 1204 that King John handed it over to the lords of Warkworth. On the attainder of the Earl of Northumberland in 1461 the lordship of Rothbury was granted for life to Sir Robert Ogle, warden of the East Marches. Although we have no record it is almost certain that the earl of Northumberland would erect a fortress in the important manor of Rothbury. Camden described it as a "brave castle" which tradition says stood on the Haa Hill (Hall Hill) the name of which is preserved in Haw Hill House. A sketch published by D. Dippie Dixon shows Rothbury Hall, the church, and bridge, with the old lock-up on the left as they appeared in 1843. The view shows that the castle consisted of a square tower with east and west gables. The prison which is often mentioned in medieval times (e.g. in 1256) probably refers to the dungeon like chambers which formed the basement of the old building. In 1661 "Rothbury Hall" was occupied by "William Thirlwall, gentleman". As late as the 1850's the upper portions were still inhabited but in 1869 the ruins were cleared away to provide an extension to the churchyard. Not a trace now remains.

ROTHBURY FOREST

The best description of Rothbury Forest is by A. Mackenzie in his *View of Northumberland* published in 1825.

"*That extensive tract of land, upon which once stood the famed* Forest of Rothbury *reaches from Thornhaugh on the east, to Fallowlees on the west, which is computed to be about seven miles; and from Coldrife on the south, to the Park-house on the north, a distance computed at four miles. The ancient trees of this* Forest, *as it is still called have long been eradicated; and those which at present grow upon it have evidently been planted for convenience and ornament. The whole is now dotted over with solitary farmsteads, from a quarter of a mile to a mile distant from one another. These houses, or rather strongholds, are very old, and are usually called* Peels. . . . *Here, however, they are named* Bastile buildings. *The walls are in general about five feet thick, and the stones secured by strong cement, though sometimes mud has been used. The doors, which are low and narrow, are usually placed at the east end of the building, the jambs of stone, with holes to receive a strong wooden bar, by which means the door was barred, and the cattle secured on the ground floor: the light was admitted through loop-holes. The second floor is supported either by a stone arch, or thick oak joists; and was entered on the south side by stone steps, the door being fastened as below. Near the fire-place, and directly above the vault door, was a projection from the wall, contrived for the purpose of pouring down boiling water on the moss-troopers, who were assailing the building below. . . . Towards the west and north-west . . . was a spacious deer-park, one mile square; the remains of the wall are still to be seen in many places. . . . The Forest is all enclosed, except a small part which joins Simonside Hills on the south-east, and a ridge of hills on the north, but which afford pasturage for sheep. . . . The extensive tract of country, called the* Forest, *has lately been much improved and beautified by the erection of many neat cottages, to each of which a plot of ground is annexed, varying in size from 12 acres to a rood."*

Not one of the strong houses described by Mackenzie remains today. In the early nineteenth century there was much smuggling carried on in Coquetdale. Scotch whisky was brought on horseback in kegs or "grey hens" over the Cheviots, and gin was brought from Boulmer on the coast. The farmer at Bushy Gap was well known in the trade as the local rhyme tells us:—

> Auld Bob Dunn o' the Forest,
> He's ridin te Boomer for gin,
> Wi' three famed horses fra Bushy Gap lonnin',
> But "Kate o' the West" is the queen o' them aa'.

His farm had a double gable and in the space between the gin was hidden. The revenue men, or gaugers as they were called, eventually discovered the secret chamber by careful measurement of the walls.

They also made their own illicit whisky locally. One still, capable of making one hundred gallons of spirit per week, was discovered in the Tosson hills in 1840. It was a sort of cavern. There was a small hole for the entry and exit of the smugglers while a spring of water, running from the hills into the cave, served for the purpose of distillation. The hills were haunted by other spirits, probably, as in Cornwall, to keep away prying eyes. The mischievous elves of the Simonside hills were called the *Duergar*.

"Many stories are told of their pranks. On one occasion, if popular testimony is to be believed, they set the huge wheel of Tosson water-mill a-going at night. Their favourite pastime seems to have been misleading travellers. One person, wandering in these treacherous solitudes, began to shout, "Tint! tint!" when a light appeared before him, at a short distance, like a burning candle in a shepherd's hut. With great care he approached, and found himself on the edge of a deep slough in a peat-bog. Throwing a piece of turf into the water, the light vanished, and as he shouted again, defiantly, "Tint! tint!" three of the elves, with hideous visages, approached, carrying torches in their diminutive hands. He betook himself to flight, and was followed by an innumerable multitude of the malevolent sprites, armed with little clubs. Charging the leader, he encountered no palpable form, and sank down in a kind of stupor to the ground, where he remained till the next morning. Another time a traveller was benighted in these parts, and perceiving a glimmering light, hastened towards it, and found what appeared to be a hut, on the floor of which, between two rough grey stones, the embers of a fire were still glowing. He had just seated himself on one stone, when a strange figure in human shape, not higher than the knee, came in and sat on the other. After remaining silently watching his diminutive companion till the fire went out and the morning broke, he perceived his danger. The roof and the walls of the hut were gone, and he was seated upon a stone sure enough, but it formed one of the higher points of a steep, rocky precipice." (Tomlinson)

THRUM MILL

The Thrum Mill stands on the north bank of the Coquet about a mile below Rothbury in a picturesque riverside setting. The Thrum is a narrow chasm in the freestone rock which forms the bed of the river. The name probably originates from the *thrum* or sound made by the rushing river. There is a saying at Rothbury "It's gan to be bad weather; hear the Thrum's roarin' ".

The Thrum is selebrated in Wilson's *Tales of the Borders*. In the story of "The Faa's Revenge" Willie Faa, the gipsy king, is represented as leaping across the Thrum with the stolen heir of Clennel Cstle,a leaving his pursuers behind. Stephen Oliver, in his *Rambles in Northumberland and the Border*, records a conversation he had with an old Coquet angler:—

"Talk o' fishing'," says he, "there's ne sic fishin' in Coquet now as when I was lad. It was nowse then but to fling in and pull them out by twees-es and threes-es, if ye had sae mony heuks on; but now, a body may keep threshin' at the water a' day atween Halystane and Weldon, and hardly catch three dizen, and mony a time not that. About fifty year syne, I mind o' seein' trouts that thick i' the *Thrum*, below Rothbury, that if ye had stucken the end o' your gad into the water amang them, it wad amaist ha'e studden upreet."

THRUM MILL.

Poaching was once very common on the Coquet. Writing in 1858 M. A. Denham described the custom as follows:—

"The *Coquet* is famous for its *Salmon*, great numbers of which are destroyed in autumn, when they ascend the river for the purpose of spawning. This used to be done with a *low* and *leister*. Formerly bodies of *Redesdale* (Rogues) and *Tynedale* (Thieves) men visited the *Coquet* for the sake of its *Salmon*. Concealment was not attempted.

The safety of the party from arrest depending upon its numerical strength and courage. Many a dismal *fray* arose out of these *nocturnal* expeditions, and fearful wounds were inflicted with the formidable instruments used in their pursuit. *The Coquetsiders* are the only men who *now* follow this illegal practice; and in favourable seasons it is to the *Rothbury Idlers* a source of considerable income; so much so, that the *payment of the rent* of their small holdings frequently depends upon the success of the *aquatic exertions*. Hence has arisen the expression—*My rent's in the Coquet yet.*"

WELDON BRIDGE

The bridge across the Coquet here carries the road from Morpeth to Wooler. Two earlier bridges were swept away in 1744 and 1752, and the present structure was built about 1760. It is well designed with circular openings in the spaces between the elliptical arches. Nearby is a famous old fishers' inn. Beyond all other places in Northumberland the haunt of fishers and once the favourite resort of Roxby, Doubleday and other poet-fishermen who with their angling songs have made the Coquet so well known. The inn has the atmosphere of the past, in spite of considerable modernization, reminding one of the old coaching houses. The bar counter, which is tiled in old Doulton, showing etchings of fishermen is worth a visit. The iron inn sign showing an angler hooking a large salmon, is a good modern example of ironwork.

> At Weldon Bridge ther's wale o' wine,
> If ye hae coin in pocket;
> If ye can thraw a heckle fine,
> There's wale o' trout in Coquet.
>
> There's wine in the cellar o' Weldon,
> If ye ken but the turn of the key;
> There are bonny, braw lassies on Coquet,
> If ye ken but the blink o' their e'e.

BRINKBURN PRIORY

The priory is in a place of perfect seclusion between the river Coquet's steep wooded banks. The name (first recorded in 1120) means "Bryrea's burn or spring". The approach to the priory is by a carriage drive along the edge of the scavers above the river. So secluded is the spot that the story is told (likewise about Blanchland) of a party of Scots who sought the place in vain. They were on their way home when they heard the bells being rung by the monks in thanksgiving for their deliverance. The Scots returned and laid waste and plundered the priory.

A Bondager (Northumbrian woman farm worker) outside "The Angler's Arms"
painting by R. Embleton

Brinkburn was founded in the reign of Henry I (c. 1135) by William Bertram I of Mitford who established there a body of Augustinian or Austin canons. The priory was originally dedicated to St. Peter only but later was known as the convent of St. Peter and St. Paul. Little is known of the history of the priory apart from the routine matters recorded in the Chartulary. The monks brought into cultivation the wastes on the high ground to the east of Rothbury and with their numerous endowments they were reasonably wealthy. In 1536 the king's commissioners visited the monastery and recorded that the canons had as a relic the girdle of St. Peter and that the prior had been incontinent with several women. The house was dissolved and the prior, one William Hodchon, was given the large pension of £11 per annum.

The remains of the Priory are considerable consisting of the church (restored in 1858) and ruins of some of the monastic buildings. The cellars and dormitory are covered by a fine 19th century country mansion. The master mason who built the priory was Osbert Colutarius. "The richest Norman work is here blended inextricably with the purest early English; and the fabric must be regarded as one of the most fascinating specimens of the transition from one to the other that there in the country." There is little ornamentation inside the church but it is very impressive with its lofty painted arches on clusters of round pillars. The doorway on the north side of the nave has a round arch ornamented with billet, dog-tooth and zig-zag mouldings, and beakhead carvings, surmounted by a triangular canopied gable with three trefoil headed arches. On the southern side of the nave is another round-headed doorway the mouldings of which are ornamented with large knots and bosses. The church is noteworthy for its lofty lancet windows, two tiers at the west end and a triple tier at the east. Among the relics preserved here are an original Norman font, a double piscina under a canopy of two painted arches, the original altar stone with five small crosses and the tomb-slab of Prior William Suffragan, Bishop of Durham who died in 1484. It is decorated with a cross-fleury, a mitre and crozier. On the lawn to the east of the church is an interesting sun-dial with many faces capped by a stone ball. In 1834 during excavations to the south-west of the church a medieval bronze pot was discovered containing nearly 300 golden Rose Nobles of Edward II, Richard II and Henry IV.

A deep part of the river near the church is called the "Bell Pool" into which the Scots on one of their raids are said to have thrown the monastic bells. The discoverer of the bells, according to tradition, will also find other treasures.

"A shady green spot in the precincts of Brinkburn is pointed out by a pretty tradition as the burial-place of the Northumbrian fairies. Their tiny forms are no longer seen in the moon-lit glade, but the flowers they loved still bloom plentifully beneath the shelter of green groves. Amongst these may be named the wood-basil, foxglove, throat-wort, woodruff, golden saxifrage, fig-wort, sweet-cicely, celandine, pellitory, toad-flax, St. John's wort, and barberry."

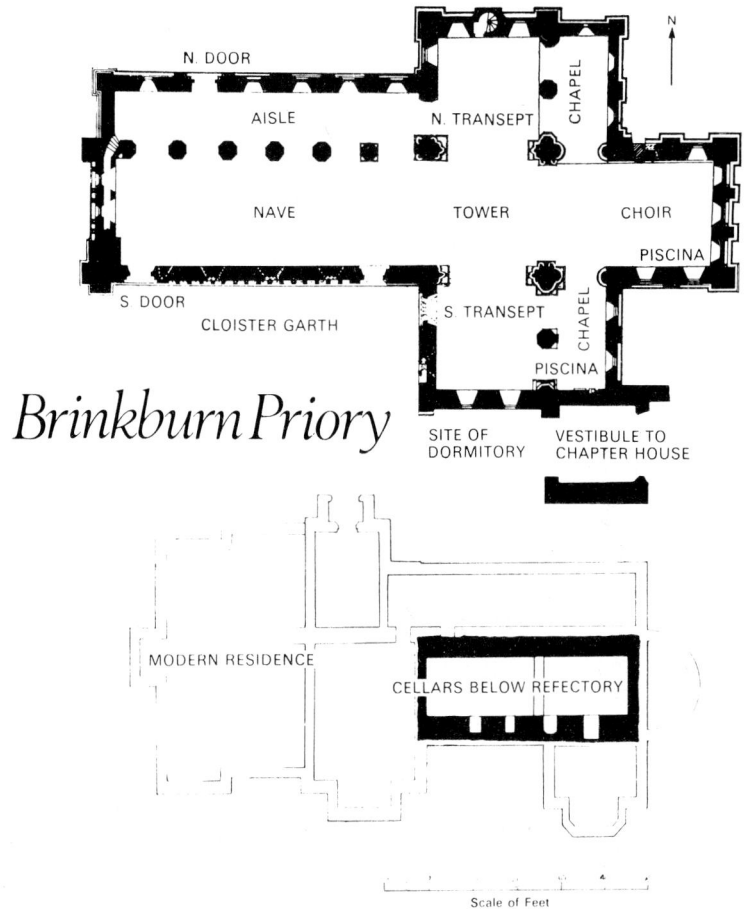

Brinkburn Priory

On the estate is *Gawen's Field*, which receives its name from Gawen Redhead, a notorious reiver who was outlawed in the reign of Queen Elizabeth. He lived in a huge hollow oak tree which was so large that 6 calves were kept inside it.

Half a mile north east but on the south side of the river is the 18th century Brinkheugh house. It belonged to the Horsleys of Long-Horsley who came to live here in the 16th century leaving their old tower. The house is stone built with five bays and two stories. The doorway has an open scrolly pediment.

Brinkburn Priory - North Door

NORTHUMBERLAND MEMORIES. £2.25. A companion volume to *Northumberland Yesteryear*.
"There is an old saying that one picture is worth a thousand words. Just how true is the adage is proved by this superb collection of old photographs, taken between 1860 and 1950 and edited by Robin Gard. Under titles varying from agriculture and shopping to mining and transport they portray a bygone way of life.

CRAGSIDE

In 1863 Sir William Armstrong visited Rothbury where he had lived as a child and decided to buy the Debdon valley. Here he built a small house called Cragside. It was in a fine romantic spot overlooking the Debdon burn. The house however was of no great architectural merit and in 1870 Norman Shaw the great Scottish architect was engaged to design a more worthy residence. The work was pushed ahead rapidly and was finally completed when a wing was added in 1880. Not everyone was pleased with the house. One critic complained: "His work was not altogether free from the somewhat lifeless Gothicism and although Cragside is considered one of the most successful of his earlier country houses, it has not the simplicity and breadth of his later work, nor is there displayed here the refinement of design and masterly handling of material which characterizes the best of modern domestic architecture". However Nicholaus Pevsner writes: "The site is Wagnerian and so here is Shaw's architecture. It has none of the *finesse* of his Chelsea houses of a few years later. What he was concerned with was high picturesqueness for his design, and he has without doubt achieved it". It is built in a composite style of architecture, partly Gothic and partly Elizabethan. There are some very fine rooms in the house. The chief entrance is in the south front through a fine Gothic doorway. The Dining Room has a huge fireplace with cosy inglenooks and an elaborate carved mantlepiece with the motto: "East or West, home's best". The ceiling is richly panelled. The Library has some very good *William Morris* glass in the bay windows.

The Drawing Room, which is situated in a part of the mansion known as "Gilnockie's Tower" is the most striking room. An enormous mantlepiece of richly carved marble reaches up to the ceiling, twenty feet high. It is said to be the work of Farmer and Brindley.

Bird's-eye view of tower &c.

Since Armstrong was an industrialist and inventor many new ideas were introduced into Cragside. It was the first private house in the country to have electric lighting. It was personally installed in 1880 by Joseph Swan an intimate friend of Armstrong. The electricity was generated by water power. Water also worked two lifts and a huge spit in the kitchen. In the conservatory fruit trees grew in huge vases which were turned on pivots by hydraulic power so that each side could receive the sun's rays in turn.

While the house was building the estate of 14,000 acres was laid out. The barren hillside was transformed by the planting of a wide variety of trees and shrubs. The guide book described it as "a veritable fairyland of fir-fringed lochs, deep and lovely gorges, idyllic walks

The three views of Cragside were drawn by R.
By permissio

Shaw and published in Buildings News. 1872.
Art Gallery

Cragside: Northumberland
Fireplace in Dining Room

. . . eight miles through a wonderland of beauty". The rhododendrons, azaleas, and other flowering trees are a special feature of the grounds. There are eight entrance gates but the principal one illustrated here is beside the "Reivers' Well".

In recent month's the present Lord Armstrong has been trying to develop the estate by building a number of expensive houses which he wants to sell to raise money to pay heavy death duties. After much controversy planning permission has been refused but the future of Cragside is very much in the balance. The cost of maintaining the grounds has become increasingly burdensome and within the next few years changes will clearly have to take place.

THE COMPLEAT COLLIER or the whole art of sinking, getting, and working coal-mines. 1708. Facsimile. 50p.

THE BLACK PUDDEN REPUBLIC by Ken Bell. £7.50. 400 pages. Controversial First Novel by Tyneside Author

The *Black Pudden Republic* is basically a world-wide adventure story, but the author himself describes it as "a tale of sex and travel, incorporating some verse on the thoughts of an English dissident".

Written in the first person by "Georgie", its anti-hero, and set in the near future, the novel carries a strong warning about the danger of democracy disappearing under the growing activities of the multi-national corporations.

But the multi-nationals and the world's oil-industry are not the only ones who might look upon the book with disfavour. The "happy Hampstead Social Democrats and half-hard Menshevik Methodists from the London School of Economics" — lumped together by the author as "the tyranny of the centre" — also come in for a slating.

One of the most brilliant and vivid characters in the book is autobiographical, describing the author's childhood days in Scotswood, Newcastle. It compares with, some might say surpasses, Jack Common's *Kiddar's Luck*.

FALLOWLEES

The name means *faw-ley* i.e. the clearing of varied colour. It lies on the slopes of Simonside. In 1541 the area is thus described:—

"There ys also greatt waste grounde southewest from the Ryver of Cockett foranenst Rothebery and stretcheth all waye southewest from a mounteyne or hyll at the northe west syde and a plenyshed countrye called the brede of Northumberland upon the southeast syde—some parties of the mountaynes or hylles hereof bene full of rockes stones and cragges, and the soyle or grounde there of blacke covered with heathe and lynge unproffyteable for pasture. In this waste towarde the northest parte thereof there ys a parcel of grounde Falloly burnes which as measurable good for pastures". Sometime after 1541 a bastle was built whose foundations can still be traced.

Large heaps of slags found along the sides of Fallowlees Burn prove the existence of early smelting works. At Fallowlees farm-house William Veitch, one of the outlawed Covenanters in the time of Charles II, lived for a time. At the request of the Redesdale people he came with his wife and children to "a village called Falalies, farming a piece of ground from Charles Hall, who was owner of that place and village within the parish of Rodberry. But they were not well settled there, though in a moorish retired place when their Roman Catholic neighbours, who abounded there did stir up the Lord Witerington to mar some small meetings he had". However they were not successful and he obtained a licence to preach.

In 1705 the Halls sold Fallowlees to Sir William Blackett who built a shooting box called Blackcock Hall near Selby's Cove. It was burnt down in 1812 by a party of gipsies. It has been suggested that this was revenge on the Trevelyans. For twenty years earlier in 1791 three gypsies had murdered Margaret Crozier at her house on Elsdon Moor. They were known to frequent some empty cottages at Swindon in Hepple township. In the following year Walter Trevelyan of Netherwitton with other magistrates turned out the gypsies and burnt down the cottages and the burning of Blackcock Hall was probably their revenge.

Blackcock Castle - Simonside.

PAUPERHAUGH

Three miles down the river from Rothbury the Coquet is spanned by a picturesque stone bridge at Pauperhaugh. In 1120 the name is spelt *Papwirthhalgh*. The name means "haugh by Papworth".

HOLYSTONE

The small village of Holystone stands on the south bank of the Coquet. Nearby runs the Roman road from Redesdale to the Devil's Causeway. The name (O.E. halig-stan) means holy-stone. Leland tells us "some hold opinion that at *Halistene* or in the River Coquet thereabout over 3000 were christened in one day". The belief is probably a misreading of Bede who tells us that one Easter Day 627 Paulinus baptized King Edwin in St. Peters (*Sancti Petri*) Church at York not at *sancta petra* i.e. Holystone.

There are two holy wells here one called St. Mungo's (the name was only used after the publication of *Rob Roy*) and St. Ninian's called today the "Lady's Well". It is owned by the National Trust and lies a quarter of a mile north west of the village. It lies in a grove of firs. Passing through a rustic arch one approaches a large basin whose sides are lined with modern stone work. In the centre stands a tall cross which was placed there just over one hundred years ago which bears this inscription—"In this place Paulinus the Bishop baptized 3000 Northumbrians, Easter 627". At one end of the pool is a statue, intended for Paulinus, which was brought here in 1780 from Alnwick. The name Lady's Well is not found in any document before the Reformation. It could refer to the canonesses of Holystone Nunnery or might have no religious connotation like the Ladies Drive at Rothbury.

The nunnery at Holystone was established about 1150 by one of the Umfravilles. It appears to have been an Augustine house (not Benedictine as is often stated). In the tax returns for 1291 there were 27 nuns in the convent, with four lay brothers, three chaplains and a master (the number 27 is so large it is probably a mistake for 7). But by 1313 the Bishop of Durham issued an appeal on their behalf describing their desperate plight—"by reason of the hostile incursions which daily and continually increase on the march, (their house) is frequently despoiled of its goods, and the nuns themselves are often attacked by the marauders, harmed and pursued and put to flight and driven from their home, and are constrained miserably to experience bitter suffering. Wherefore we make these things known to us, that you may compassionate their poverty, which is increased by the memory of happier things, and that your pity and benevolence may be shown them, lest (to the disgrace of their estate) they may be forced publicly to beg".

The nunnery was dissolved in 1535 and the seven nuns pensioned off at 40s. each. The conventual buildings seem to have been destroyed after 1541 and the stone used for extensions to Harbottle Castle. The Church of St. Mary, restored in 1848, stands on the site and some fragments of carved stone work, relics of the convent, have been built into the walls. In the outside wall of the chancel are three incised tomb slabs with ornamental crosses.

On Dove Crag burn is a pretty little waterfall and lower down the stream is *Rob Roy's Cave*—a dark opening beneath a huge cliff accessible only by a narrow path. It was a traditional hiding place of the famous outlaw. Above the cave is a large Celtic camp with a double rampart and dry ditch.

At Holystone is a fine old hotel called The Salmon Inn, with an old stone fireplace. At the back of the fireplace is a hidden cavity probably not a priest's hole but used for hiding smuggled goods.

PEELS

Probably the only interesting thing about this hamlet is its name. It lies on the north bank of the Coquet near Harbottle. It was not the site of a tower but part of the lands of Harbottle Castle which was enclosed by a fence or *paling*. The two words pele and pale are closely connected and were probably pronounced almost the same.

HEPPLE

The village of Hepple lines the magnificent road which runs from Rothbury to Elsdon. Hepple was held by means of a form of personal service, Celtic in origin, known as *drengage*. The earliest thegn whose name is known was Waltheaf, whose son William was thegn in 1161. The pele tower here was built in the 14th century. It was the first of a line of towers, extending to Warkworth, which formed a barrier against Scottish invaders. The shattered remains can be seen beside the main road (See *Castles of the Aln and Coquet*).

Half a mile west of Hepple is Kirkhill on which there once stood a chapel which was destroyed by the moss troopers. The remains were removed in 1760 to help build nearby West Hepple farmhouse. In the chancel they found a tombstone which is said to have had the following inscription which is quoted by Mackenzie:—

"Here lies . . . Countess of . . .
. . . who died . . . her age
. . .
I loved my lord, obeyed my king,
And kept my conscience clear,
Which Death disarmeth of his sting,
And Christians all endear.

My puissant posterity
Still the forlorn'd befriend;
Peace, pleasure, and prosperity
My tenantry attend.
. . .
There lay my head to Long Acres,
Where shearers sweetly sing,
And feet toward the Key-heugh scares,
Which fox-hounds cause to ring.

Farewell survivors in the gross!
When you behold my bust,
Lament your late liege lady's loss,
Then blending with the dust."

How much of this inscription is invention we do not know.

One hundred yards from the site of the chapel are traces of the village of *Old Hepple*, destroyed by the Scots, probably at the same time.

The modern Hepple church was built in 1897. In it is a Norman carved font bowl from the old chapel. Beside it is the head of a cross which stood beside the moorland track near Paunchford. Built into the wall nearby is a tombstone with three horse-shoes below a floral cross.

Two noted Northumbrian characters are connected with Hepple.

"Hepple was the native place of the renowned Robert Snowdon, who, in his sixteenth year, fought and slew John Grieve, a celebrated Scotch champion, in a pitched battle with small swords upon 'Gamble Path', at the head of Coquet. This circumstance appears to have taken place before the Union—1603. This Robert Snowdon had a black horse which he greatly prized. It was one night stolen, when he, accompanied by two friends, pursued the thief to the Scottish borders, where, from a wretched hovel, his voice was answered by the neighing of his favourite, on which the unsuspecting Snowdon dismounted and rushed into the house, but while in the act of unloosing his horse, he was run through the body by a concealed assassin. The family of the Snowdons were all distinguished for their intrepidity and dexterity in the petty feuds of those turbulent times". (Mackenzie).

The second character was Will Allan a famous vermin-hunter and performer on the Northumbrian Pipes. He was the composer of two tunes, "We'll a' to the Coquet and woo" and "Salmon tails up the water".

CLENNELL

There is now no village at Clennell. It was cleared away in 1895 to provide park and gardens for Clennell Hall. This country residence built in Tudor style, incorporates an old pele tower and Elizabethan hall. Clennel stands near an important highway called Clennell Street which joins the Salters' Road just before the Scottish Border. It was the main road into Kidland during the Middle Ages and later an important drovers' road. Clennel is first mentioned in 1181. The name means "Clean Hill" that is free from trees.

The family of Clennell took their name from the place. In 1228 the monks of Newminster made an agreement with Thomas of Clennell for wayleave for their cattle to Kidland during the months of summer. From that time Clennell has remained in the hands of the same family although the descent has not always been on the male side.

The countryside around abounds with remains of the ridge-and-furrow of medieval fields. Many are found on the slopes beneath Camp Knowe. The area was once densely populated compared with today and these cultivated terraces were once part of the vanished medieval village.

HARBOTTLE

The picturesque and historic village of Harbottle is on the south side of the Coquet in a hollow among rocky heath-covered hills. The name—*hir botle*—means the "station of the army". This Saxon village was occupied by the Umfravilles after the Conquest. One of the earliest village records tells us:—

"In 1245, it was found, after the death of Gilbert de Umfreville, the famous baron, that, in the manor of 'Hyrbotl,' there were 408 acres and 3 roods of land, worth, at rack rent, 5d. an acre. Item. 98½ acres of meadow, of which, 20 at rack rent, were worth 6d. an acre, and 78½, worth 2d. Item. Two mills, worth the yearly rack rent of £17 11s. 4d. Item. A borough, which, with the herbage, yielded a rent of £2 12s. 0d."

Harbottle Castle was built about 1160. It stands on a steep hill overlooking the river on one side and the village on the other. The castle is now a ruin. We have written its history in our booklet on *The Castles of the Aln and Coquet*.

After circling the castle the river makes a curious bend which is known as the "Devil's Elbow". The *Border Survey* of 1604 tells us "the town of Harbottle was sometimes a market town, and the tenants there inhabiting claim to be free burghers." However the unsettled conditions prevailing here during the Middle Ages prevented the development of town life.

A footpath from Harbottle past the Presbyterian manse leads up Harbottle Hill to the famous Drake Stone, a huge reddish-grey sandstone rock nearly 30 feet high. The massive boulder is the Draag Stone of the Druids and the custom once prevailed of passing sick children over the stone to help their recovery, a pagan custom similar to passing them through fire.

The Drake Stone

A hundred yards to the south-west is Harbottle Lough a lonely tarn with pure water which is always bitterly cold. Tradition tells us that there were once plans to drain the lough but when the workmen arrived they were panic stricken when they heard the following warning coming in sepulchral tones from the middle of the tarn:—

"Let Alone; Let Alone!
Or a'll droon Harbottle,
An' the Peels
An' the bonny Hallystone."

ALWINTON

This quiet little village lies at the junction of the Alwin and Coquet. The name means "farm on the Alwin". Here was once a hospital attached to the nunnery of Holystone. The original settlement was probably at Low Alwinton where the old church of St. Michael stands. It is the junction of two important tracks called "Clennel Street" and the "The Street" which can easily be traced and followed today. In 1887 James Hardy wrote:—

"*Alwinton lies in an angle among the green meadows and cultivated enclosures at the foot of Paspeth. Instead of the picturesque village with the houses disposed in all sorts of positions which we saw in 1868 the houses are now in regular ranks and mostly newly erected . . . The inns have been renovated. The old dwellings had oak-frames which were fastened to the ground, and upheld the wattled and thatched roofs.*"

However the visitor today will find little uniformity but an unspoilt northern village. The Red Lion was rebuilt in 1903. It is now a store. Of the Rose and Thistle, Paul Brown wrote in 1937:—

"The illustration of the inn parlour is from a sketch made some years ago before the swell fireplace was put in. It is a quaint room typical of the smaller old North-country inns before they sprouted lounges, cocktail bars, and bathing pools. It is a homely room, its old beams, old settle, thick old walls and stone floor give it character and its window affords a view of a charming garden."

One distinguished visitor to the Rose and Crown was Sir Walter Scott who came here to gather material for Rob Roy.

ALWINTON CHURCH

Alwinton is the first of the Ten Towns of Coquetdale. They are Alwinton, Biddlestone, Clennell, Chirmundesden, Sharperton, Farnham, Burraden, Netherton, Fawdon and Ingram. They were probably joined together in Saxon times and their function was to support Harbottle the military centre.

Alwinton is famous for its Annual Sheep Show usually held early in September. In former times there were also horse races and a football match played in the true Northumbrian manner between the men of Redewater and the men of Coquet.

The Church of St. Michael was originally a Norman edifice but was greatly altered in the early English period and rebuilt in 1851. Since the church stands on a steep slope the nave is separated from the chancel by a flight of ten steps. The 13th century south transept is the mortuary chapel of the Selbys of Biddlestone Hall. The north aisle is the resting place of the Clennels or Harbottle and contains two massive 18th century altar-tombs. At the west end is a pointed bellcot whose bell is rung from a rope hanging outside.

In the neighbourhood of Alwinton are many ancient remains. On Windy Gyle is Russell's Cairn a prehistoric mound of stones which was later named after Sir Francis Russell who was killed nearby in 1585 on a day of truce while a Border meeting was in progress. On Gallow Law is a contour fort, at Wholehope and earthwork on Dryhope Hill prehistoric hut circles. Early cultivation terraces can be found at the Lord's Seat and Sharperton.

NETHERTON

The road from Thropton through Snitter passing Trewhitt House leads to the small village of Netherton (Nedertun 1050—meaning "lower farm"). Like most Northumbrian villages it has declined in size during the past century. It was once one of the "ten towns of Coquetdale". From here a road two miles long leads to Biddlestone Hall or the main road can be taken to Alwinton 5 miles away. There is an inn here called The Star.

SNITTER (Snitere 1176)

The old English word *sniteren* means "to snow". Perhaps its exposed position gave it this name. It stands on a ridge three miles north-west from Rothbury. Dixon tells us that the Half Moon Inn here was in former times a great centre for cock-fighting and card-playing when legs of mutton were the favourite prizes. The Half Moon is now gone.

WARTON

One and a half miles west of Thropton is Warton, now a mere farmhouse with cottages. The land here is very rich and it was called the *Core of the Coquet*. At Warton farm Robert Spearman reared the famous West Kyloe Ox which when slaughtered in 1835 weighed over 200 stone. Known also as the "Warton Ox" it was often exhibited in the Border towns.

Mackenzie (1811) tells us "this place is famed in the legendary tales of the neighbouring inhabitants as being the residence of a choice race of warriors, who were the dread of the Scottish borderers. Even so late as the middle of the last century four brothers lived here of the name of Potts, who usually kept the peace at all public sports when there was ill-blood between the people of Coquet and Redesdale".

FLOTTERTON

It is called *Floteweyton* in 1160. It means a "settlement by a road over a marsh". Here in 1416 a tower is mentioned but nothing more is known about it although it may have been on the site of the present Flotterton House, a fine country house built in 1826 by Christopher Wealleans.

THROPTON

The large village of Thropton lies two miles west of Rothbury on the road to Harbottle at a point where the Wreigh burn joins the Coquet. The land here is fertile and the inhabitants used to be called *Tatey Town Folks*, because this was the first place at which potatoes were grown in this part of the country. The saying is used as a *reproach*.

In the early part of the nineteenth century a cross was standing at each end of the village. One of them used to stand in front of the "Cross Keys" Inn.

Thropton Tower is first mentioned in 1415 as belonging to William Grene. In 1509 it was held by Sir Edward Radcliffe and contained a garrison of 16 men for defence against the Scots. It may have been part of Thropton Old Hall which was demolished in 1811 to make room for the Catholic Presbytery. But there still remains at the west end of the village a well preserved pele tower with walls five feet thick. It has been modernised and is still occupied. It is of two stories with a vaulted basement and an original window in the west gable shows there was always an attic. There are two original first floor windows.

Besides the Cross Keys there is the fine inn called *The Three Wheat Heads*.

WHITTON TOWER

For many centuries it was the residence of the rectors of Rothbury. Before the first world war it was turned into a Children's Hospital which it remains today. The house now consists of the old pele with various later additions on two sides. The pele tower was built in the 14th century but the upper part was probably added by Alexander Cook who did a good deal of restoration when he was rector of Rothbury in the 15th century.

The tower is unique in having vaulted rooms on the first and second floors. The reason is that due to the slope of the ground its height changes from 42 feet on the south side to 60 feet on the north. This allowed entrance on two floors. The ground floor room has walls more than nine feet thick and the entrance has the unusual feature of two doors at either end of the passage. The well here is three feet in diameter and fifteen feet deep. Entrance to the floor above is by a square hatchway in the roof. In this first floor sitting room a large mullioned window of three lights has replaced a small opening in the south wall. A restored shoulder headed door in the corner opens on to an old newel-stair up to the second floor. This newel stair has many mason's marks and extends to the top of the tower. During alterations in 1894 a recess was revealed which may have been a secret room as well as a piscina carved with oak leaves.

Sharpes Folly
Rothbury

The tower was altered and repaired at various times and extensive additions made in the eighteenth and nineteenth centuries.

SHARP'S FOLLY

Archdeacon Thomas Sharpe was given the living of Rothbury in 1720 by his father the Archbishop of York. He dabbled in astrology and erected a round tower at the higher end of the grounds as an observatory to carry on his pursuits. He also claimed it was to relieve unemployment among the village masons. Although not beautiful it is an example of fine workmanship. It was soon called "Sharp's Folly", although the term is not strictly accurate since in the eightventh century the word *folly* simply meant any fanciful building intended for ornament rather than use.

Also in the grounds is a fine sun-dial erected by Dr. Sharpe.

Brinkheugh

BRINKHEUGH

Half a mile to the north east of Brinkburn Priory, on the other side of the river is the beautifully situated house of Brinkheugh. It is a five bay two storey building with quoins. The doorway has an open scrolly pediment. It was the home of the Horsleys of Longhorsley as early as the reign of Elizabeth. The house as we see it today is probably early 18th century. Weldon Hall which was nearby was taken down some time before 1900. It was described in 1750 as "well adorned".

CARTINGTON CASTLE

Cartington Castle stands three miles NW of Rothbury controlling the Debdon pass over the Rothbury hills. It is first mentioned in 1415 and in the Survey of 1541 is described as a "good fortresse of two toures and other stronge houses". In the reign of Elizabeth extensive alterations were carried out making it one of the largest and finest mansions in Northumberland. It suffered badly during the Civil War but was subsequently restored. In the 18th century it is referred to as a "handsome seat on the top of a hill well planted with trees" but before long it became a ruin. In 1887 Lord Armstrong had the remains strengthened and preserved. The architect C. C. Hodges has been criticised for his work, perhaps unjustly, but some of the windows were probably never in their present positions. It is now very difficult to disentangle the various stages of the building.

The castle consists of a great square courtyard with a range of buildings to the north, the east end of which is a lofty 14th century tower. This tower measures 31 x 41 feet and has walls 6 feet thick. The ground floor is a semi-circular barrel vault. The reminder of the north wing is now at ground level divided into three large rooms.

On the south side of the courtyard are two towers the south east one being the oldest and containing a guardrobe: the one on the south west is barely visible.

GREAT TOSSON TOWER

The ruins of the border tower of the Ogles stands in the centre of the village of Great Tosson nearly opposite a house which was formerly the Royal George Inn. It appears to date from the 15th century but in 1541 was reported as "not in good rep'ac'ons". It was one of a line of towers extending from Harbottle to Warkworth. It was in size 42 by 36 feet with walls 9 feet thick. Although the large outer stones have been removed the rubble interior stands solid like concrete. A very good spring is nearby and this was probably inside the barmkin.

The Rev. John Hodgson wrote the following description of it about 1830:—

"Tosson Tower. Its vault still remains but the arch of it much broken, the outside ashlar and indeed almost the whole of the inside ones except the pining stone have been taken away. The masonry is good, the wall 8 feet thick, the inside as usual rudely enough filled with line, sand and rough stone all of which are strongly cemented together, the sand porphyry from the bed of the Coquet: has a doorway to the south east. Behind it on the south rises one of the Simonside hills which prevents the sun from shining upon it for nearly 3 months in the winter: to the north-east it has a fine view down upon Rothbury, Whitton Tower, Newtown, Thropton, Trewhit and the fertile and undulating land from Biddlestone to Rothley and from Snitter to the Cheviots. Thus Tosson stands proudly and darkly over the valley, has some trees about it: the stone of which the vill and tower are built excellent white sandstone".

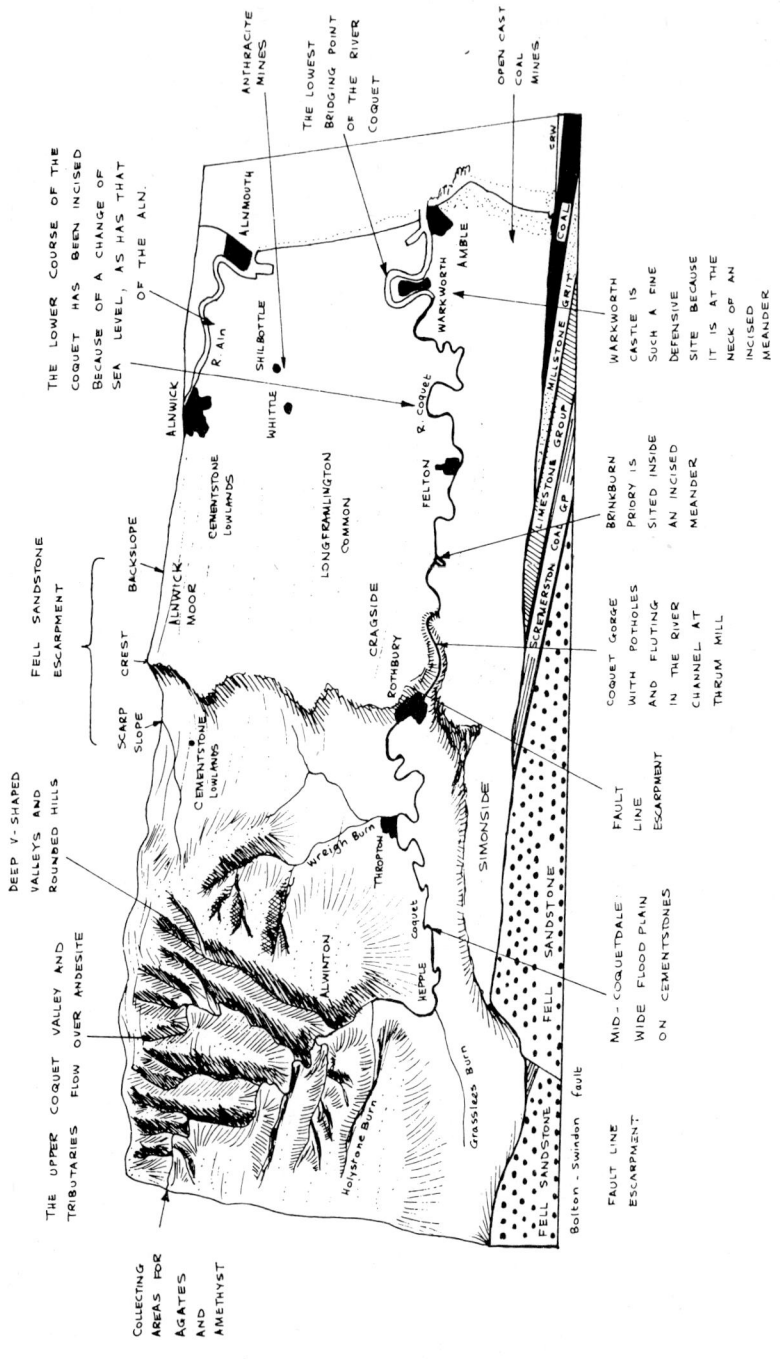

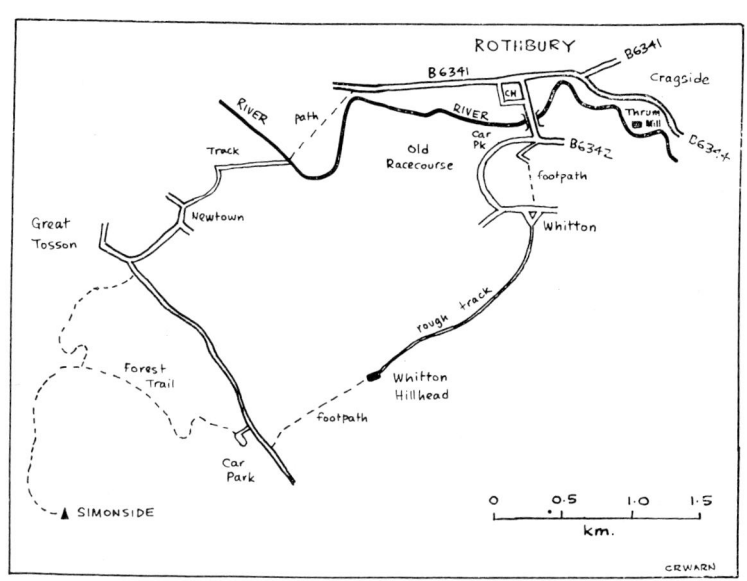

A GEOLOGICAL WALK FROM ROTHBURY TO SIMONSIDE

C. R. Warn

Rothbury can be reached by the B.6344 from Morpeth, the B.6341 from Alnwick, the B.6342 from Hexham, or on the 416 bus from Newcastle and Morpeth.

Rothbury is a settlement with a population of 1,800 people and is a local market centre with considerable appeal to the tourist. This is partly because of its siting, as it is enclosed by a horseshoe shaped ring of hills formed from resistant Fell Sandstone, a deposit of coarse grained deltaic sandstone laid down in the lower carboniferous period (about 325 million years ago). The open end of the horseshoe faces westwards, and the lowland is there because the bedrocks are soft cementstone series deposits which have been easily eroded to form a broad vale called 'Coquetdale'. To the East, at Thrum Mill, the River Coquet cuts through the Fell Sandstone in a dramatic gorge. The river is still actively eroding its bed by processes of attrition whereby pebbles moved by turbulent eddy currents scratch out potholes and fluting lines. Before setting out for Simonside, it is well worth going to Thrum Mill to see this, and also to gain a glimpse of the famous Cragside gardens, renowned for their Rhododendrons that thrive so well on the acid podsol soils derived from the Fell Sandstone.

Leaving Rothbury, one should cross the Coquet by the bridge on the B.6342 and turn right immediately afterwards to follow the minor road that runs beside the river. The car park and the former racecourse are both located on alluvial deposits of the Coquet flood plain. The road curves southwards and climbs up the 'buff line' of the river valley past the cemetry to a road junction where one turns left and continues climbing to Whitton Stables. Here an unsurfaced track leads south westwards beyond Witton Hillhead to the Simonside Forest entrance. The gentle climb along this track affords excellent views over coquetdale and enables one to distinguish between the gentle, rolling landscape of the shales and limestone of the Cementstone Group and the harsh, craggy landscape of the Fell Sandstone. The boundary between the two types of rocks occurs roughly at the point where the farmland ceases to be enclosed. On reaching the minor road at 038996, turn right and continue the short distance to the entrance to the Forest Trail on the left, which is clearly signposted.

The walk to Simonside Summit is simply a matter of following the signs along the track. In the forest section there are many ditches which give excellent soil sections through the podsol and peaty—gley-podsol soils that are so characteristic of the Fell Sandstone. When above the treeline, the more natural vegetation cover of bracken, heather and cotton grass is seen. Often there are patches of bleached white sand where the bedrock has been broken down into granular fragments by weathering. Simonside itself is formed from a series of inclined beds of hard rock tilted gently to the south to give a north face that is both steep and stepped. The scarp slope of the hills are difficult to ascend in places, and reveal cliff like rock exposures that show current bedding structures. These indicate that the rocks were laid down by huge rivers draining into a delta from the Cheviot Massif to the North West.

The views from Simonside are very good in all directions. To the North West are the Audesite and Granite rocks of the Cheviot Hills. The red coloured quarry at Biddlestone can be spotted also. It is the source of the red Felsite rock that is used so frequently for roadstone in the neighbourhood. The view westwards shows a continuation of the Fell Sandstone escarpment through Ravens Heugh and Tosson Hill, until being displaced by a powerful fault that runs along the line of the Grasslees Burn. To the south is a much lower landscape formed predominantly from sandstones, limestones, shales and coal deposits belonging to the Limestone Group. The boundary between the Limestone Group and the Fell Sandstone deposits is very sudden, and this is because of a fault which runs South Eastwards from Pauperhaugh. To the north of course lies Rothbury, to which a return can be made via Great Tosson (030005). This hamlet is reached either by forest track or by returning to the car park and proceedings along the minor road. In Great Tosson are the remains of a limekiln that once used the limestone from the cementstone deposits. From here one can descend to Newtown (035010) and then cross the river by a footbridge, from which a path leads across the flood plain to the B.6341. This road follows the line of a large fault which brings the Fell Sandstone outcrop as far west as Snitter. The return to Rothbury is simply a matter of following the B.6341 to the East.

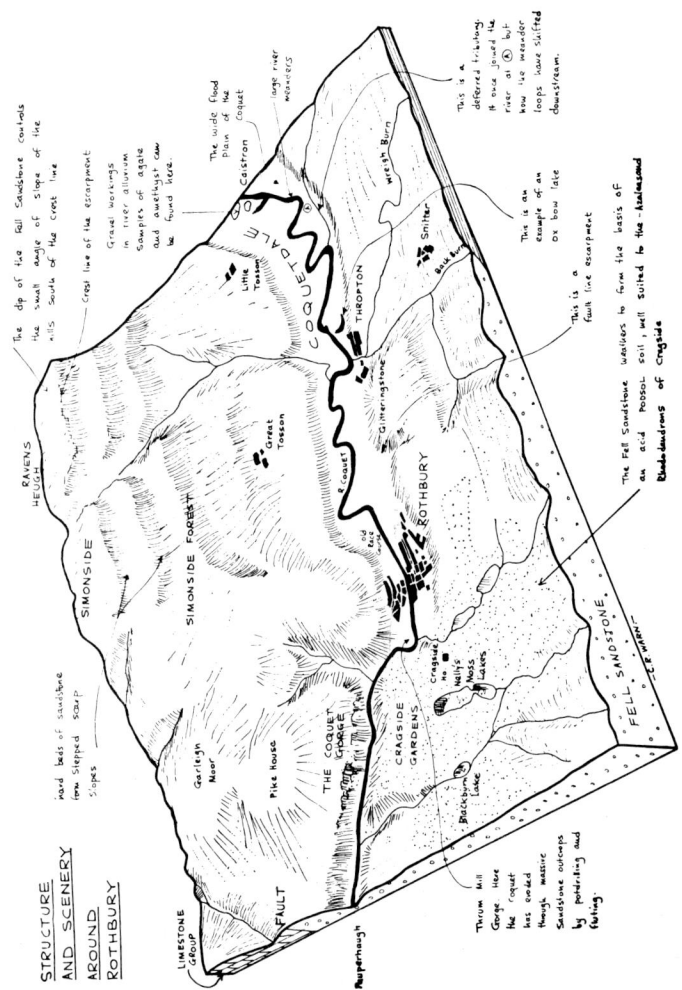

COQUETDALE SAYINGS

The pea kytes o' Coquet
The sheakle meakers o' the Woodside

These two sayings are mutually used as terms of reproach; and the following observations will illustrate their origin. That portion of the vale of *Coquet* adjacent to *Woodside*, is agricultural, whilst the other is, almost exclusively, pastoral. The vale of *Woodside* abounds in natural wood, and the facility with which it is obtained, has induced the custom of twisting *birch twigs* in a peculiar manner, to serve instead of hempen bands for the purpose of tying up cattle. These are called *sheakles* (shackles); hence the expression.

Rothbury Thrum will be the ruin of us all

A little to the east of *Rothbury* the *Coquet* flows through a narrow gorge with precipitous rocks on each side. When the river is swollen the whole of the bottom, which consists of solid stone, is covered with water; but in dry seasons the flow is restricted to a channel some XV. feet wide, scoped out of the rock by the powerful and long continued action of the stream. Here the confined current, surging and foaming, flows with great rapidity. It is said to have been formerly of much less width; but on one or two individuals having been drowned, in attempting to leap across, the rock was cut away, to prevent a repetition of the experiment. Such is the place familiarly known as *Rothbury Thrum*.

The above expression is, or at least was very common amongst the seamen on the *Thames* (!) and this affords another instance of a *local saying* travelling far from the place of its origin. About XXXV. years ago a Mr. *Taylor*, from the neighbourhood of *Rothbury*, was stationed near *York*, as an excise officer. During one of his rounds, he was accosted by three fellows soliciting charity in the character of *shipwrecked seamen*. On enquiry where the dire disaters had happened, he was told in *Rothbury Thrum*. Pleased to hear the name of a place with which he had been familiar in boyhood, Mr. *Taylor* gave them a shilling, with the admonition, never more to make the *Thrum* the scene of their calamity.

My rent's i' the Coquet yet

The *Coquet* is famous for its *Salmon*, great numbers of which are destroyed in autumn, when they ascend the river for the purpose of spawning. This used to be done with a *low* and *leister*. Formerly bodies of *Redesdale* (Rogues) and *Tynedale* (Thieves) men visited the *Coquet* for the sake of its *Salmon*. Concealment was not attempted. The safety of the party from arrest depending upon its numerical strength and courage. Many a dismal *fray* arose out of these *noctural* expeditions, and fearful wounds were inflicted with the formidable instruments used in their pursuit. The Coquetsiders are the only men who *now* follow this illegal practice; and in favourable seasons it is to the *Rothbury Idlers* a source of considerable income; so much so, that the *payment of the rent* of their small holdings frequently depends upon the success of their *aquatic exertions*. Hence has arisen the expression—*My rent's in the Coquet yet.*

The Core of the Coquet

Warton, a township in the parish of *Rothbury*, is famed in the legendary tales of its inhabitants, as having been the residence of a choice race of warriors, who were the dread of the *Scottish Borderers*. The above characteristic is spoken of the land in this locality, in token of the superiority of its soil. Reprinted 1973.

These sayings have been taken from the "Denham Tracts", or a few Pictures of the Olden Time in the North of England." written and published by M. A. Denham in 1846. Reprinted 1973.

GENERAL INFORMATION

Accommodation. Coquet Vale Hotel, The Turk's head Hotel, Newcastle House Hotel, Bonahaven Guest House, Railway Hotel, Orchard House, Queen's Head Hotel. The Anglers' Arms, Weldon Bridge. Three Wheat Heads Inn, Thropton.

Area. 167,886 acres, population (1969) 5,160.

Early Closing Day. Wednesday.

Administration. Rothbury Rural District Council.

Fishing. Licences and permits from J. R. Soulsby and Sons, Front Street, Rothbury.

Caravans. Coquetdale Caravan Park Ltd., Bridge Street, Rothbury.

THE HISTORIAN OF COQUETDALE

It would be inappropriate to write a history and guide to Coquetdale without some mention of *David Dippie Dixon* the famous historian of the area. His book — *Upper Coquetdale* — recently reprinted, is a local history classic.

David Dixon was born in 1842, the eldest son of the village draper at Whittingham. When David was twenty his father opened another shop in Rothbury and the family went to live there. For six decades David lived at Rothbury and was almost eighty when he retired from business. He died in 1929 at Cragside Farm on Lord Armstrong's estate whose librarian Dixon had been for a number of years.

The first of David Dixon's two major books, *The Vale of Whittingham*, appeared originally in a slighter version, privately printed, and then, in full, in a *de luxe* edition of two hundred numbered copies, in 1895. The subscribers' list included eight of the Dixon family, one of them George in Australia. There was no need to publish the second book, *Upper Coquetdale*, by subscription, for its predecessor had established a public for the writer. Both books were well illustrated by David's brother, John Turnbull Dixon, an accomplished artist, with pen drawings of buildings and landscapes, an occasional wash drawing, and Bewickian vignettes at chapter ends. Robert Redpath of Newcastle published both books.

Naturally, local histories are superseded in time by later versions, with benefit of new research, excavations and discoveries, and the historical passages of these two books have necessarily suffered from this progress. It is noticeable, however, that the relevant volumes of the *Northumberland County History* (xiv, 1935; xv, 1940) draw heavily upon the Dixon books of four decades earlier. Equally, these books cannot be used as contemporary topographies or guides, for land usages, agriculture and scenic features have changed, society has been modified, and buildings have come and gone during the last seventy years. However, the loss on the swings has been more than matched by the gain on the roundabouts. Dixon's books have become historical documents themselves, describing for us the two valleys, the way of life and some of the personalities alive or not long departed, as the last century ended.

Indeed, this is the great charm and value of these two books today — the passages that people the countryside for us, and provide the humanity which ought to clothe the bones of history. Where else may we readily encounter the Kidland shepherd and his ways, the Windyhaugh schoolmaster, the hang-over from the ancient Debatable Lands quarrels, and "Sir Burn" who, whip in hand, drove his fugitive daughter back to her husband? Such persons and such events were part and parcel of David Dippie Dixon's Northumberland in all its rich variety, and he, thoughtful fellow, has handed the essence of them on to us, who have to rummage around at length to find personalities and events standing out of the ruck of our more humdrum society and daily life.

(From Roland Bibby's introduction to reprint of *Upper Coquetdale*)

NORTHUMBERLAND AND DURHAM. A Social and Political Miscellany. 200 illustrations. £6.75.

A CORNER IN THE NORTH. Yesterday and Today with Border Folk. by Hastings M. Neville. 1909. Facsimile. £2.50.

HISTORICAL NOTES ON CULLERCOATS, WHITLEY AND MONK-SEATON by W. Tomlinson. 1893. Facsimile. £3.50.

SMUGGLERS AND POACHERS AT WALLINGTON HALL. Fascinating facsimile of a recorded incident in 1830. 50p.

BOURNE'S HISTORY OF NEWCASTLE 1736. £18.

GEORDIE SONGS, JOKES AND RECITATIONS. 60p.

A LANG WAY TO THE PANSHOP by Thomas Callaghan. A vivid down to earth account of growing up in Benwell, Newcastle, in the Thirties. A worthy successor to Kiddar's Luck. 112 pages. £1.50.

NEWCASTLE SILVER by Dr. Margaret Gill. £1.50.

ROMAN COOK BOOK. 70p.
Our Geordie Cook Book has become famous and has gone into several editions. Our Roman Cook Book will probably attract similar attention. Lavishly illustrated.

WHITTINGHAM VALE, its history, traditions and folk lore, by David Dippie Dixon. 1895. Facsimile. £7.50.

NORTHUMBERLAND FARE by Margaret Slack. £1.20.
This is a little gem of a recipe book but also a fascinating essay on social history. We are treated to the *original* versions of recipes for such delights as singin' hinnies, leek pudding and pan haggerty, and the more aristocratic Duke of Northumberland Cake. But author Margaret Slack is not only a cook but a social historian. She gives a fascinating glimpse into the lives of working and upper class families of the last century, including their basic diets and weekly food budgets.

THE LIFE OF BILLY PURVIS. The Famous Geordie Comedian. 1875. Facsimile. £2.50.
"Billy Purvis (1784-1853) was the most famous clown and jester the north has ever known. His acting became a legend in lands between the Tees and Tweed. His life is not only the story of a great actor and comedian but also a social history of the area. In it we meet a way of life, methods of entertainment and an industrial and rural society which has now passed away." The first life of the great clown called *Life and Adventures of Billy Purvis* was written by J. P. Robson and published in 1849. Other editions followed. The present biography was published by T. Arthur in 1875.

THE
HISTORY
OF
NEWCASTLE *upon* TYNE:
OR, THE
ANCIENT *and* PRESENT
STATE
OF THAT
TOWN.

By the late *HENRY BOURNE*, M. A.
Curate of ALL-HALLOWS in NEWCASTLE.

—— H*æc* —— *alias inter Caput extulit Urbes* —— VIRG. Ecl. I.

NEWCASTLE upon *TYNE:*
Printed and Sold by JOHN WHITE. M.DCC.XXXVI.